# The Complete Book of

# Stenciling

## Furniture Decoration & Restoration

# The Complete Book of
# Stenciling

## Furniture
## Decoration
## & Restoration

## PAT MIDKIFF

DRAKE PUBLISHERS INC. NEW YORK · LONDON

## Acknowledgments

I would like to express my appreciation to the Shelburne Museum, Inc., in Shelburne, Vermont, for providing the photographs in the book. My visit to the museum and its Stencil House was an experience I shall always remember.

A very special thanks to Paula and Bob Bergens of the World of Arts and Crafts, Tampa, Florida. Their help was invaluable.

Published in 1978 by
Drake Publishers, Inc.
801 Second Avenue
New York, N.Y. 10017

Library of Congress Cataloging in Publication Data

Midkiff, Pat.
  The complete book of stenciling.

  Includes index.
  1. Stencil work. I. Title.
TT270.M53    745.7'3    77-88949
ISBN 0-8473-1668-8

Printed in the United States of America

*To a very special lady,*
  *Jessica M. McCormack, my Mother.*

# CONTENTS

# PREFACE

Most stenciling books belabor the mechanics of stenciling and don't provide the ideas and actual patterns. Stenciling, in itself, is a simple procedure. I have tried to provide clear, concise instructions and a full selection of patterns. If you can make a stencil and apply the paint or powders, you can decorate anything.

Read the techniques and the instructions carefully before starting any project. Buy the needed supplies, and plan the project in advance. Start by doing the easier designs first, and you will soon be doing the most difficult ones.

The most significant aspect of stenciling is its low cost. You can transform a $10 chair into a priceless addition to any decor. Decorate a child's room with several of the whimsical animals for the cost of a few jars of acrylic paint. Wallpapering the same room would cost much, much more. A simple skirt and blouse can be stenciled for $15 as opposed to a $50 or $60 similar purchase in a boutique.

For example, the skirt in this book cost $6 plus one-half yard of elastic and the paint I already had; the jersey top cost $1. The whole outfit came to $20. For a one-of-a-kind outfit, the cost is minimal.

Antiques are lovely, but if they aren't pretty and well cared for, they can detract from your home. Stenciling can transform them into an attractive addition. The antique washstand that I stenciled for this book is used as a storage cabinet in our den. I bought the stand at an antique fair for $15. I don't know its true age, although I was assured it was very old. The most important thing to me was the fact that it suited my needs. I can honestly say that, for very little money and a little time and energy, I have solved the storage problem in our den.

What I like best about stenciling is that it creates an original article.

*Pictures courtesy of The Shelbourne Museum, Shelbourne, Vt.*

# INTRODUCTION

Stenciling can be traced back to early Egyptian and Oriental cultures. In fact most civilized people throughout history have used stenciling in one form or another for decorative purposes. French and English stenciled wallpaper imported by colonial Americans became the inspiration for stenciled walls that are recorded in Early American decorations. Decorating with stencils is the art of restoring and reproducing antiques.

Webster defines stencil as: "a thin sheet, as of paper or metal, perforated in such a way that when ink, paint, etc. is applied to the sheet, designs, letters, etc. form on the surface beneath the sheet." Simply put, it is a technique in painting, using patterns, allowing even the novice to produce beautiful pictures and decorations. The stencil designs in this book help accomplish this end.

Most of the stencil patterns we see today were used in Early American decorating. The early settlers brought the art of stenciling from England and used it to reproduce a favorite wallpaper pattern to use in their new homes. Borders along ceilings and baseboards and around fireplaces were the most popular ones until overall patterns became stylish.

One of the most readily recognized stencil motifs used today is the Pennsylvania Dutch variety. These colorful patterns are used to decorate furniture, walls, floors, and a myriad of other objects. One of the most popular pieces is the familiar "hex" sign. It is hung on houses and barns and has made a tremendous resurgence in recent years. In reality, these stencil patterns have been traced back to Germany and did not originate in Holland.

Another recognizable stencil is found on the Hitchcock chair. These chairs were produced in Connecticut between 1812 and 1853, but they have been copied all through the years and are still being copied today.

The secret to any art project is patience; rushing the steps will only make the work more difficult. The better the equipment you use and the finer the supplies, the more successful the project will be.

Practice before you tackle the real thing. Use a piece of poster board to get the feel of it. Varnish it and watch it closely because it will dry much faster than on wood. Practice using all the steps. When using the different types of paint, try various consistencies to see which gives a better result.

One of the most impressive examples of Early American stenciling is the Stencil House at the Shelburne Museum in Shelburne, Vermont. Walking into this beautiful house gives you the feeling of being transported back into time. The museum has many other examples of stenciling and shouldn't be missed if you are in the area. The two pictures appearing on page 10 are only a sampling of this beautiful art.

Many of the patterns in this book are antique reproductions. Some are classic and easy to recognize. Others I have made up and drawn myself. A design should reflect your taste and needs. I have included many basic pieces to enable you to do this. I have always been fascinated by old patchwork quilt patterns. I make my own quilts and am always on the lookout for antique ones. The quilt designs I'm familiar with are the basis for most of my geometric patterns. These old patterns can be used in both modern and antique settings.

Color is another very personal thing. Some people are more comfortable with soft understated colors; others are happier with a bold vivid effect. All of the patterns can be tailored to your own taste. One of the most stunning effects I have seen was a light, frothy, gold leaf pattern stenciled on dark wood paneling. It formed borders along the ceilings and floors and around the doors. The effect was beautiful. It enhanced the wood grain and patina and relieved the darkness.

Although it doesn't take an artist to perfect the art of stenciling, the finished product might well be considered a valuable treasure. With antiques becoming more scarce and more expensive each year, amateur collectors should concentrate on creating their own. Stenciling is one way to accomplish this. You don't have to be a master craftsman. This book is written for the novice who wants clear, concise and easy-to-follow instructions with good results. You can even make up your own patterns. Be creative and let your imagination be your guide.

# Part I

## Chapter 1

## SUPPLIES AND TOOLS

### Graph Paper

In order to place a pattern properly on a large area, such as a wall or a floor, use graph paper as shown in Figure 1. Scale down the pattern, and work out the placement and the corners.

*Figure 1  Graph placement*

Use graph paper to reduce or enlarge a pattern to fit your own particular needs. To begin, block off the pattern using the number of squares corresponding to the area and size desired. Copy the pattern in each block exactly as on the squared-off pattern. Number the squares as in Figure 2 for easier copying.

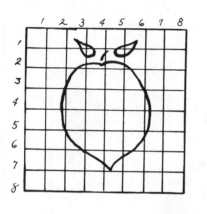

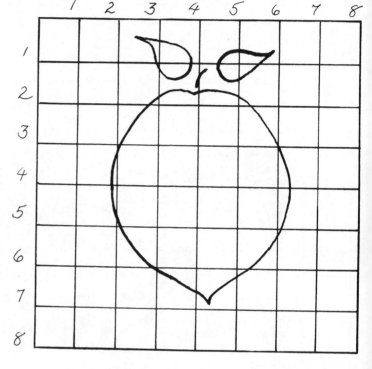

*Figure 2   Reduce or enlarge
a design*

## Graphite Paper

Graphite or carbon paper is used to transfer the traced drawing to the stencil or template. When using graphite paper, use paper clips to hold traced pattern and graphite paper securely to stencil material. Once you have started to transfer the pattern, movement of any of the parts can cause distortion on the completed design. If movement should occur accidently, remove the graphite paper, and line up the tracing to that part of the completed transfer. Holding the sides of the two materials securely, slip the graphite between them and reclip. You can now proceed with the transferring process.

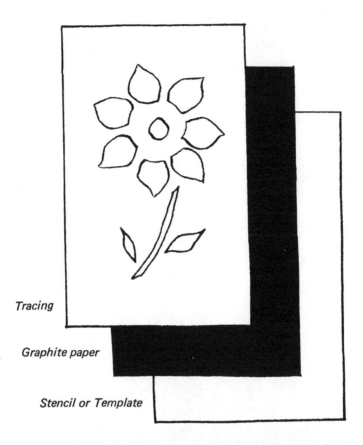

Figure 3 Tracing graphite paper, stencil, or template

### Tracing Paper

Any thin onion skin paper will do. When tracing the pattern from a book, use a sharp pencil and try to be as accurate as possible. The small details on each stencil are very important to the overall picture.

### Stencil or Template

This can be sheet acetate, heavy waxed stencil paper, architect's linen or artist's canvas that has been treated. I use the stencil paper and architect's linen for furniture because it is easy to cut and manipulate. The architect's linen is available where decoration supplies are sold. Artist's canvas can be bought by the yard at craft stores. I use the sheet acetate any time a stencil is to be used repeatedly. If care is taken when using the sheet acetate, and it is cleaned and dried after each use, it will last indefinitely.

### Knives

Any sharp knives that are found in craft stores, such as X-Acto knives, are good. They have extra, replaceable blades and come in various shapes. The sharper the blade, the easier and better the results. I use a medical scalpel with replacement blades. It is extremely sharp and must be handled with a great deal of caution. Be especially careful when replacing the blades.

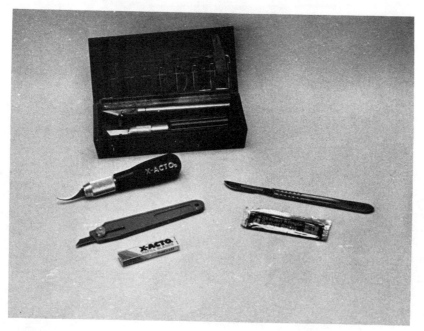

*Figure 4*

### Scissors

Small manicuring or art scissors with straight
blades work best.  I have two different sizes.
Whenever you have a straight line in a stencil
pattern, cut a single cut with the knife and
trim both sides with the scissors.  Using the
scissors gives you more precision in cutting.
In addition a pair of regular scissors for
cutting is necessary.

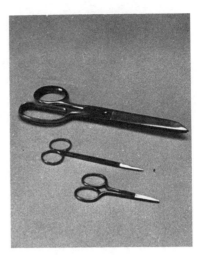

*Figure 5*

### Metal-edged Ruler

Use the ruler as a guide for tracing and cutting straight lines.

### Punches

I use a variety of old dental tools in different sizes for the very fine
holes and a leather punch for the larger ones.  A leather punch can be
purchased in craft stores.  There are two different types of punches.
One is a hollow metal tube with one end sharpened to a razor's edge,

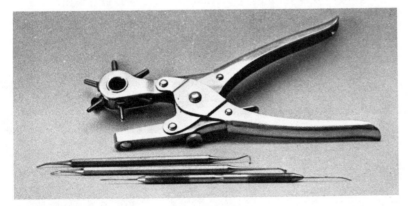

*Figure 6*

and the other has a hand grip and makes different size holes. Both are tapped with a small hammer to punch out the holes. These tools are great to have, but are not necessary to cut out stencils. You can cut them out with your knife, but special care must be taken for accuracy.

## Varnish

Any good quality, clear, wood varnish can be used on furniture. Be sure it is clear varnish because the wood stain will cloud the stencil art. I use Deft's satin finish Defthane. It is a clear polyurethane finish that needs very little rubbing and gives a mellow, satiny, antique look.

When varnishing a floor, use a hard finish polyurethane floor varnish. This affords protection against wear. A special note when varnishing over a stencil: sometimes paint will bleed when varnish is applied over it, especially red paint. Test it beforehand to make sure. If the color bleeds, apply a coat of shellac first. Depthane polyurethane varnish does not make the acrylic paint bleed.

## 4-0 Steel Wool

Steel wool is used to buff the glossy finish when working with varnish. This procedure will also give you the mellow, satiny, antique look. To buff, gently rub the layer of varnish. You must do this gently so as not to penetrate the varnish and mar the stencil picture. All you want to do is to remove the shine from the varnish.

## Turpentine

For quick and handy cleanups, saturate a cloth with turpentine, and store it in an airtight jar for repeated use. Use turpentine for cleaning brushes after using oil-base paints and varnish. (Plain water can be used to clean brushes after using acrylic paints.) Turpentine is also used as a solvent to thin oil-base paints.

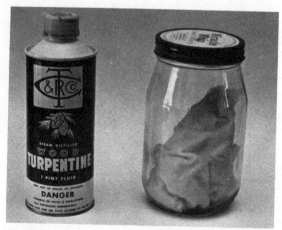

*Figure 7*

*Figure 8a*

## Brushes

Stencil brushes come in many sizes and qualities. Remember, the better the equipment you use, the better the job you will do. You need at least three different sizes of the stenciling brushes. You need one brush for each color used in each size, but this may be extravagant when first starting. Therefore, I suggest one in each of the following sizes: small, medium, and large. It is very easy to clean the brushes when you need a color change. After cleaning the brushes, dip them in benzine (lighter fluid) for quick drying.

You will also need a good varnish brush.

When stenciling on fabrics, use an assortment of regular stiff bristle brushes in addition to the stenciling brushes.

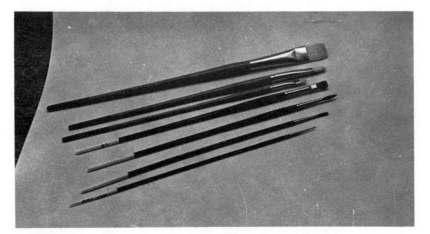

*Figure 8b*

## Velvet Bobs

Cut 1½-inch squares of deep pile velvet. Place the velvet square wrong side up, and place a ball of cotton in the center. Hold down the cotton with the head of an old-fashioned nail (2 or 3 inches in length). Pick up the sides and corners of the velvet and secure around the nail with a small rubber band to form a velvet balloon.

Make as many bobs as colored powders used. Keep a few extra bobs handy to use for highlighting.

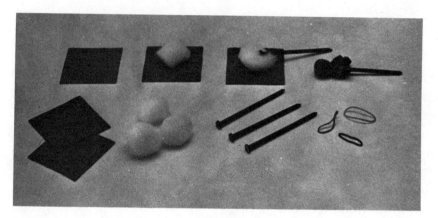

*Figure 9*

## Paint

There are many types of paint available for use in stenciling. This chart will give you some idea as to their characteristics:

| TYPE | FINISH | RESULT |
| --- | --- | --- |
| acrylic tube | matte | fast drying |
| acrylic liquid | shiny | fast drying |
| acrylic jar | matte | fast drying |
| oil tube | shiny, vivid | very slow drying |
| enamels | shiny, vivid | slow drying |
| Japan colors | bright | super fast drying |
| textile paints | bright | slow drying |

Note: When Japan drier is added to oil-base paints, it does hasten the drying time.

White paint can be added to Japan colors to give them a faded antique look.

You must choose the medium that best suits your project and your ability to work with it. Experiment with the different kinds before you start. Different consistencies may make one easier for you to work with than another.

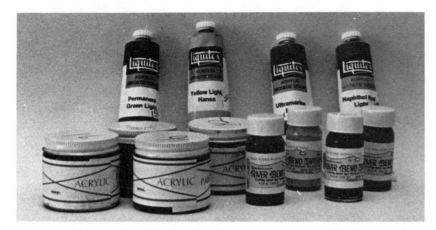

*Figure 10*

**Bronze Powders**

The powders available for stenciling come in many shades. Bright Gold, Rich Gold, Copper and Fire Gold are just a few. These colors, alone or combined, should be sufficient to do any projects in this book. The best powders are called *lining* powders because they are very fine and blend well.

*Figure 11*

### Cutting Board

I use an old-fashioned bread board with several layers of newspaper over it to cut stencils on. The newspapers protect the board from getting cut and marred, giving you an uneven surface to work on. Any board or a piece of Masonite can be used.

### Lava Soap

When using Bronze powders, use Lava soap to clean the surface of the project where powders have dropped accidently or where they have feathered around the edges. A gentle washing with Lava soap and water will lift the powders. Place a clean cloth, dipped in the Lava soap and water, on any sharp instrument, and use the point to get around the edges.

### Masking Tape

Use masking tape to hold stencils in place or to cover portions of the stencil not to be painted.

When stenciling for the striping effect, measure carefully and stencil all four corners. Let dry thoroughly. To finish, use masking tape to join stripes, completing pattern. Paint or apply bronze powders between the strips of tape. You will achieve straight, clean stripes.

*Figure 12  Tape holding stencil*

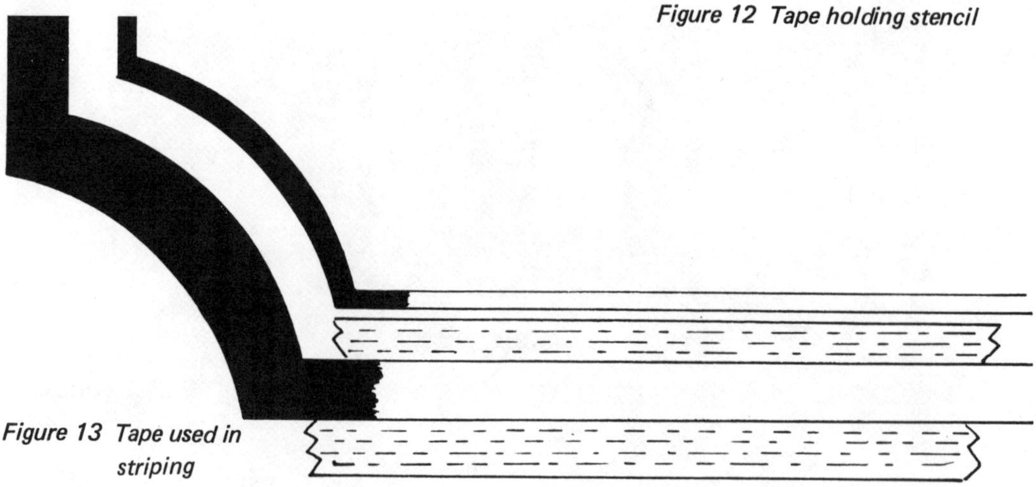

*Figure 13  Tape used in striping*

**Blotter**

A blotter should be placed under the fabric when stenciling to absorb excess paint and prevent the paint from bleeding into the surrounding area.

**Chalk String**

A chalk string should be used when stenciling floors for straight lines and placement.

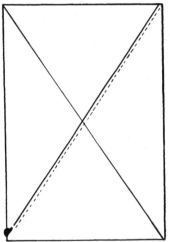
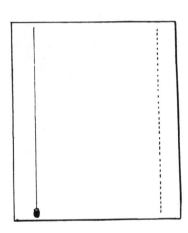

*Figure 14  Floor - chalk lines
Lift chalked string and snap gently*

*Figure 15  Wall - plumb line*

**Plumb Line**

For straight lines and placement when stenciling walls, a plumb line should be used.

**White Marking Pencil**

To mark dark surfaces for stencil placement, use a white marking pencil.

**Dark Marking Pencil**

To mark light surface for stencil placement, use a dark marking pencil.

Stripping areas

*Figure 16  Marking light on dark surface*

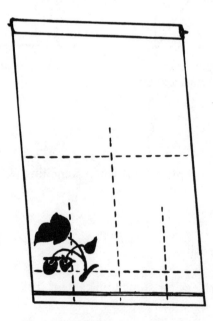

*Figure 17  Mark dark on light surface*

**Koh-i-noor Drawing Pen and Ink**

To mark waxed or acetate stencils for placement and for register marks on both, Koh-i-noor ink is used with Koh-i-noor drawing pen.

*Figure 18*

**India Ink**

This is used in straight pens with removable points.

**Mitering**

Mitering is easier with a piece of paper folded to a 45-degree angle. Keep it handy when placing stencils on surfaces.

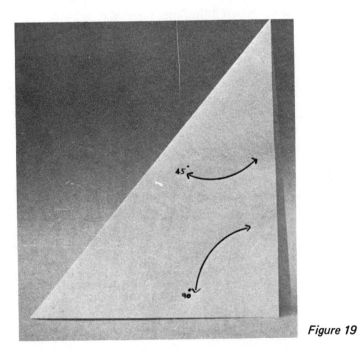

*Figure 19*

## Chapter 2

## TECHNIQUES AND INSTRUCTIONS

### Choosing a Pattern

The first step in making a stencil is to choose the appropriate design for the project at hand. In the pattern section of this book, there are designs in all categories, to suit most needs. Many individual patterns will enable you to make up your own designs. Use these as stepping stones for your own creativity. A good place to get ideas and designs is from fabrics, wallpapers, and the new designer sheets that are available.

### Single Stencil Procedure

Start by using a single stencil procedure. This is the process of stenciling using one single stencil. Walls, floors, and allover patterns use one basic stencil. Simple furniture stenciling can be accomplished with one stencil, also. An allover pattern, such as a wall or floor, uses the same basic stencil over and over. When doing this type of stenciling, use sheet acetate in making the stencil. Stencil paper and archi-

*Figure 1 Single stencil*

*Single stencil repeat*

tect's linen sometimes becomes soggy at the edge of the cuts from repeated applications of paint. The acetate can be wiped clean, dried and used again immediately.

## Multiple Stencil Procedure

Furniture stenciling is usually a multiple stencil procedure. Often in stenciling you will find a flower or a bird that is two or more colors, and the colors are not separated by a bridge. As shown here, for instance, a separate stencil is used for each color. A bridge is that part of the pattern between the cutout parts. It is sometimes referred to as a separator.

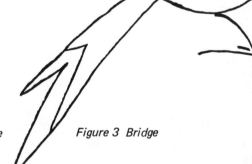

*Figure 2 Not separated by a bridge*      *Figure 3 Bridge*

## Your Own Design

When making up your own stencil to form your own design, start by choosing a base and flower shapes, stems, and leaves that you will need. Trace each item that you want from the pattern section of the book onto a master sheet. On a second sheet, retrace and place each item in its proper place. When you transfer to the stencil itself, you can make last minute corrections to the overall picture. Broken lines are used in each succeeding stencil to indicate placement and color change.

*Figure 4  Multiple stencil; cut three stencils; cut only on split lines*

Another method of making up a design is the single pattern repeat. As shown here, a simple design can be transformed into many different patterns.

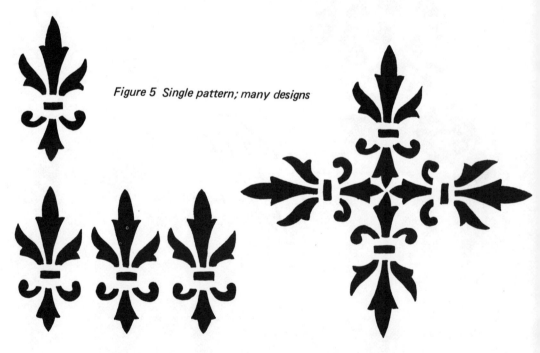

*Figure 5  Single pattern; many designs*

The next step is transferring the pattern to the stencil paper. Using graphite paper, trace the pattern by pressing firmly over each line with a sharp pencil until the complete pattern has been covered. Be sure to include every detail. The small markings are essential to the overall picture.

## Cutting the Stencil

Using an X-Acto knife, hold the stencil firmly and exert enough pressure to cut through the stencil material. Draw the X-Acto knife toward you when you make the cuts. Cut all of the vertical cuts and turn the stencil 45 degrees and finish cutting. A single line in a

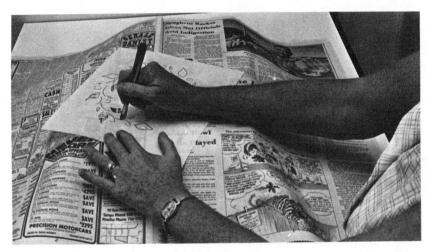

*Figure 6*

pattern should be trimmed on both sides with small scissors to make them more pronounced. The last thing to do when cutting out a stencil is making the holes where indicated. Use a leather punch or dental tools. When the holes have been completed, turn the stencil over and trim the rough edges of the holes with scissors.

Another method of cutting stencils to achieve a smooth cutting edge is to move the stencil, not the knife.

*Figure 7*

## Preparing the Surface to be Stenciled

The surface of furniture should be refinished or painted well in advance so that the piece is completely dry. Rub down the finish with 4-0 steel wool and wipe clean before applying varnish if you are going to use powders.

Walls should be washed or painted, and floors should be painted or varnished before stenciling.

Fabrics should be washed to remove all sizing and finish before stenciling.

All surface areas should be marked for stencil placement before starting.

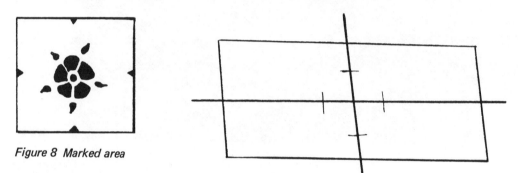

*Figure 8  Marked area*

## Paints

Personal taste and final effect should determine the medium to be used. Try the different types of paint beforehand to see which works

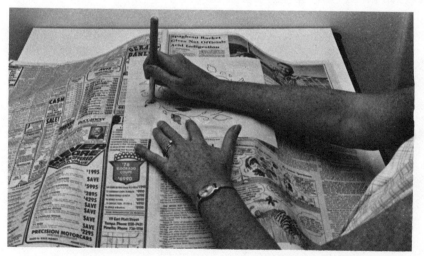

*Figure 9*

best for you. Use the information in the section on supplies and equipment.

When using paints, keep the following points in mind:

Tape the stencil with masking tape to keep it in place.

Tape over those areas where bridges are narrow or thin and where paint may stray.

When using paints with stencil brushes, dip the brush into a flat paint holder, such as a paper plate, and then tap the brush on an old newspaper to disperse the paint evenly over the bristles and to dislodge the excess.

Stencil painting is accomplished with repeated dabs of the brush in an upright position, as shown in Figure 9.

It is better to go over an area a second time to achieve the color needed than to use too much paint the first time. Too much paint on your brush can cause the paint to seep under the edges of the stencil and smear.

## Cleaning the Stencils

It is very important to keep the stencils free of excess paint. Use a damp cloth when cleaning up acrylic paints, and use the turpentine cloth that you prepared ahead and stored in the jar for the oil-based paints. A buildup of wet paint can cause smearing when lifting and replacing a stencil. A dried buildup can cause distortion of the design.

## Wipeout Procedure

Wipeout and fading can be accomplished by dipping a small paint brush in solvent and actually wiping the central area until some of the stencil paint comes off. This procedure leaves the background paint or finish showing through, and the overall effect is faded.

When using oil paints, use turpentine as a solvent.

## Powder Technique

The powder technique is a little more difficult. Highlighting, shading, and using one or two basic powders takes practice. Using your poster board, take one pattern part, such as a leaf, and practice.

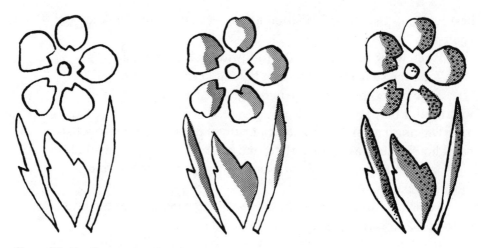

*Figure 10 Shading and highlighting*

A black or dark background should be used with this technique to contrast with the metallic powders.

Varnish the surface area to be stenciled. Let dry until it is tacky. This tackiness is what the powders adhere to. Sometimes when an area is large, it is better to varnish and stencil one half of the area at a time.

Powder stenciling is accomplished by rubbing the stencil area with the fine bronze powders, using the velvet bobs. A circular motion, when applying powders, is the most successful. Use a separate bob for each color powder used.

Immediately after applying powders, clean the surface areas, where powder has dropped accidently or where the edges have feathered, with Lava soap and water.

After the powders are applied and highlighting and shading have been accomplished, let dry overnight.

Next, wash the whole area that has been stenciled with warm water and a very mild soap. This removes any loose powders and prevents smearing when final coat of varnish is applied.

## Painting on Fabrics

The first step in stenciling on fabric is washing the fabric to remove the sizing and the finish.

The new acrylic paints work well in this medium. Place many layers of newspapers on top of your work area, and place a large blotter in the center. Place that portion of the material to be stenciled on the blotter. Tape the stencil into place with masking tape. Proceed with painting the stencil pattern.

Paint is applied in the same manner as in doing furniture, dabbing the fabric with the stencil brush. Too much paint will cause the colors to bleed into the surrounding areas, so be very careful. It is better to repeat the application to get the desired color depth than to use too much paint the first time. Let each application dry thoroughly. When changing colors and using multiple stencils, let each color dry, also.

## Setting Color in Fabrics

After acrylics have dried on the fabric, heat your iron to medium setting (wool — no steam) and cover with a clean dry cloth and press. Press for two or three minutes on each side. This sets the paint. Rinse the fabric in a solution of half vinegar and half water. Now the garment can be laundered repeatedly without damage to the stenciling. I recommend washing by hand. You can put hand-painted articles in the dryer but just long enough to remove the wrinkles.

## Sponge Technique

This technique is carried out much like the others but gives a slightly different effect.

Tap the sponge on a newspaper to remove excess paint, and dab the surface to be stenciled. Variations in design can be achieved by swirling and wiping with the sponge. A sponge brush, available in craft stores, or a fine nylon sponge work well with this technique.

*Figure 11 Sponge technique*

## Register Marks

When making a stencil for a border or a design to be repeated in sequence, mark the stencil. This mark or guide allows perfect placement of the design. On paper or canvas stencils, you can mark with ink. On plastic or acetate, the marks must be made by notching the stencil.

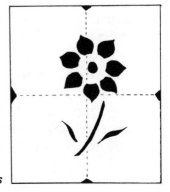

*Figure 11a Marked stencil, regular notches*

## Turning Corners

Plan the turn of a corner before you cut the stencil. You can use the continuous or broken method. The continuous method is accomplished by literally curving the pattern and not breaking the design.

The broken method stops at the corner, intercepts the design, and continues along the next side. In this method, the corner is stenciled separately.

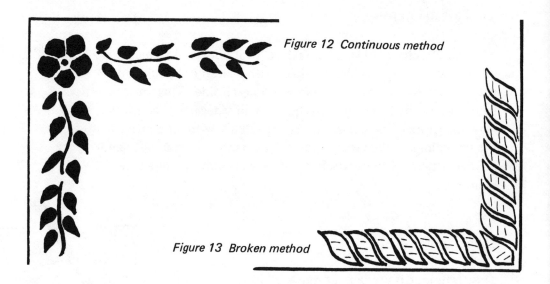

*Figure 12  Continuous method*

*Figure 13  Broken method*

## Care of Stencils

When doing a large area, such as a floor or wall, and using the stencil over and over, I suggest using sheet acetate because it can be wiped clean and dried immediately. Paper and canvas stencils become wet and ragged.

If a stencil is not abused, it can be filed away for future projects. A library of precut stencils can save you much time in your next endeavor.

When making stencils, write the colors to be used on each one. This can help to avoid mistakes.

Proper care of all tools and equipment will enable you to continue stenciling with very little expense in the future.

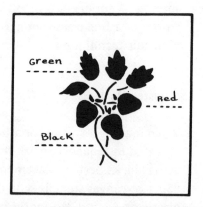

*Figure 14  Color reminders on stencils*

## Chapter 3

## PROBLEMS AND HOW TO SOLVE THEM

*Feathering* — In working with powders, sometimes the edges of the stencil become ragged. This can be caused by too much powder on the bob. These edges can be cleaned up with Lava soap and water.

*Working on curved wood* — Using architect's linen for your stencil enables better placement.

*Bleeding* — One color runs into another. Let each color dry before adding another. When varnishing over a stencil, test the paint first. A coat of shellac before the varnish will alleviate this.

*Varnish* — If it is too dry or too wet, you will have trouble with powders.

*Smudges* — Special care should be taken when lifting the stencil. The slightest slip will smear the project. Too much paint on the brush, or brushing toward the outside of the cut rather than toward the center will also cause smudges.

*Breakdown of the stencil* — Sometimes the bridge of the stencil is very thin and breaks when you are using it. If so, use tape and repair immediately. If the stencil has to be used repeatedly, it is better to recut a new stencil.

*Unsharp edges* — This is caused by too much paint on your brush or a stencil that is wet and soggy because of the medium you are using. An acetate stencil would solve the problem.

*Smeared powders* — When applying varnish over stenciled powders, be sure to wash with soap and warm water first.

*Faded look of colors* — When applying paint, use two or three applications to achieve color. Too much paint in one application causes smears and bleeding.

*Knife hard to control when cutting* — Replace blade. A sharp blade cuts a clean edge.

*Problems with shading* — Shading is most successful when lighter shade of base color is applied while surface is still wet.  This allows blending.

*Overlapping* — Bridge of stencil is too narrow.  Use masking tape to enlarge bridge.  If the stencil is to be reused, and the gap is too large, recut the stencil.

*Drying of paints* — As you work with the different mediums, you will soon learn to recognize when the paint is getting too dry.  When working, keep turpentine and water handy to correct consistency.

*Clogging of designs* — If you are diligent in keeping the stencils wiped clean, you can avoid this.

*Saturated brush* — When using oil-based paint, use a paper towel saturated with turpentine to rub brush clean.  When using acrylic paint, wash brushes with warm soapy water, rinse well, and dry with paper towels.

*Crooked placement* — Marking the area to be stenciled and marking the stencil itself will avoid this.  Plumb lines on walls and chalk lines on floors are necessary.  On small flat areas, a T-square is a great help.

*Abrupt endings* — Register marks on stencils and working out the complete pattern, scaled down on graph paper, helps.  Work out the endings and turns beforehand.  The time you spend working out problems before you start is time well spent.

# Part II

Part II

Project 1:

## ANTIQUE HITCHCOCK CHAIR WITH BRONZE POWDERS

*STEPS*

1. Finish or paint surface of chair to be stenciled.
2. Select stencil patterns to be used.
3. Make stencils.
4. Varnish area to be stenciled. Watch closely to determine tackiness.
5. Place stencil by using appropriate guidelines, and tape into place with masking tape.

*Figure 1*

6. Using velvet bobs, apply powders in a circular rubbing motion. Work on cutouts in stencil one at a time.

*Figure 2*

7. Highlight and burnish edges; shade.
8. If edges are feathered or a bit of powder has dropped, clean up surface area with Lava soap.

*Figure 3*

9. When completely dry, after overnight, wash stenciled area with mild soap and water.
10. Varnish over the stenciled area to protect it. Let dry again overnight.

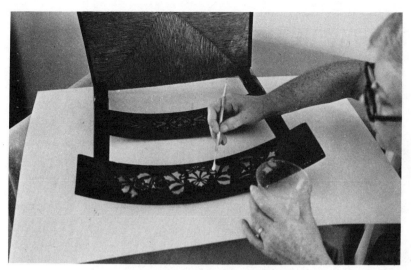

*Figure 4*

11. Rub down with steel wool for mellow finish.
12. Revarnish and rub down again.
13. Painting gold bands on the legs of the chair is called stripping.
14. Varnish over stripping on legs, and rub down with steel wool.

*Figure 6*

*Figure 5*

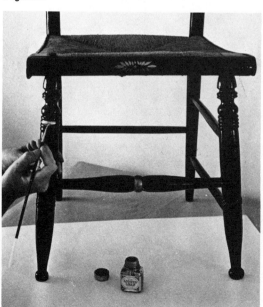

# WASHSTAND WITH PENNSYLVANIA DUTCH DESIGNS

Figure 1

*STEPS*

1. Paint or refinish washstand.
2. Select and make stencils.
3. Wipe surface with a clean cloth to remove dust.
4. Place stencil by using appropriate guidelines, and tape into place.

Figure 2

*Figure 3*

5. Apply paint and move stencil to next area to be stenciled.
6. Let dry thoroughly.
7. Apply borders and stripping.

*Figure 4*

8. Varnish and let dry thoroughly.
9. Rub down with steel wool.

*Figure 5*

# PARSONS GAME TABLE

Figure 1

*STEPS*

1. Paint or refinish table surface. White, satin finish enamel is an attractive choice.

Figure 2a

*Figure 2b*

2. Choose pattern and make stencils.  A geometric design for the top and a decorative design for the sides and legs are good ideas.
3. Mark table top and sides for stencil placement.  Tape stencils in place with masking tape.
4. Stencil in same manner as in painting procedure.  Use black acrylic paint to contrast with the white background.

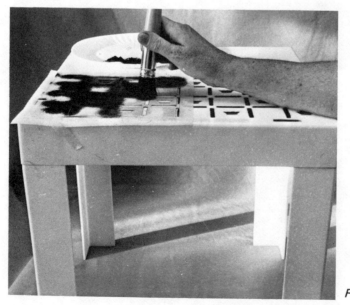

*Figure 3*

5. Stencil legs of table in same manner.  Be careful when lifting stencil to proceed to the next area.
6. Strip bands to form border by using masking tape.

*Figure 4*

7. Let dry thoroughly.
8. Apply Depthane polyurethane varnish.  Do not rub down table with steel wool because a smooth semi-glossy finish is desired.
9. Checkers or chess pieces can be placed to complete project.

*Figure 5*

---

# STENCILING ON FABRICS

---

Figure 1

*STEPS*

1. Wash fabric to remove sizing and finish.

Figure 2

2. Prepare work area.
3. Make stencil.
4. Arrange stencil on fabric and tape into place.
5. Apply paints and let dry.

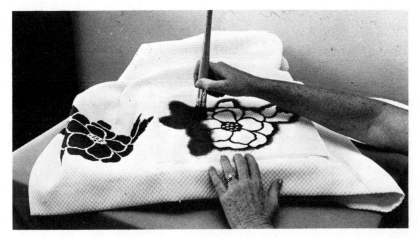

*Figure 3*

6. Repeat if more vivid colors are desired.
7. Let dry thoroughly.
8. Press with dry cloth to set paint.
9. Rinse in vinegar and water solution, and let dry.
10. Press.

*Figure 4*

**Project 5:**

## WINDOW SHADE

*STEPS*

1. Wipe the shade clean to remove surface soil.
2. Choose and make stencils.
3. Mark off area to be stenciled, and secure stencil in place with masking tape.

*Figure 1*

4. Apply first color to stencil, and lift stencil carefully. Let dry. This surface should dry quickly if you are using acrylic paint.
5. Move the stencil to the next position and continue, in this case, with the green leaves.

*Figure 2*

6. Let dry thoroughly.
7. Now, reapply the stencil over the first stencil of leaves, and continue doing the strawberries in the second color, red.

*Figure 3*

8. After all the paint has dried, apply tiny dots to strawberries for authenticity with a very fine tipped brush.
9. Let dry thoroughly.
10. Spray a very fine mist of Decoupage finish over the whole painted area.

*Figure 4*

**Project 6:**

## WALLS AND FLOORS

Stenciling walls and floors is an art in itself. It can be an enormous money-saving decorating approach to the new home owner, or it can be a means of adding authenticity to restoring and decorating an older home. For either reason, it can add charm and beauty to your surroundings.

Once you have mastered the art of simple stenciling, walls and floors can be the ultimate challenge. Your choice of pattern and design will determine the difficulty and extent of the job.

When doing a large area such as a wall or floor, make a master stencil with several repeats of the pattern in width and in length. This will save much time in lifting and moving the stencil to the next area.

Start with a basic motif, and build on it with other patterns. Work out the size of the area to be covered and the size of the master stencil. Plan the project well to ensure success. Refer to Figure below.

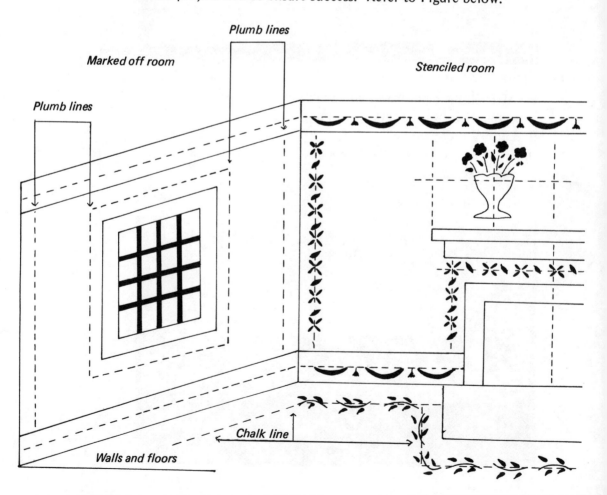

## STEPS – WALLS

1. Prepare the surface.
2. Use plumb line and ruler to mark off wall.
3. Do a scaled down drawing of the area to be stenciled. Choose the stencils to be used. Make proper placement on the scaled drawing and make adjustments.
4. Tape the stencil into place and apply paint. Be very careful when lifting the stencil to go on to the next area. The slightest shift will smear the paint.
5. Clean the stencil.
6. Using the register marks on the stencil, replace the stencil and continue.

## STEPS – FLOORS

1. Prepare the surface.
2. Use chalk marker to mark off floor.
3. Make a scaled down drawing on graph paper and place design, as in doing the walls.
4. Stencil the floor in the same manner as the walls.
5. When all the stenciling is completed and has dried thoroughly, varnish the floor with several coats of polyurethane varnish.

**Suggestions for Projects**

old furniture
window shades
lampshades
walls
floors
clothing
curtains
toy chests
trunks
note paper
Christmas cards
tiles
paneled doors
wall headboards for beds
valances
canvas on director's chair
monograms
tennis shoes
T-shirts
game tables
shower curtains
kitchen cabinets

# Part III

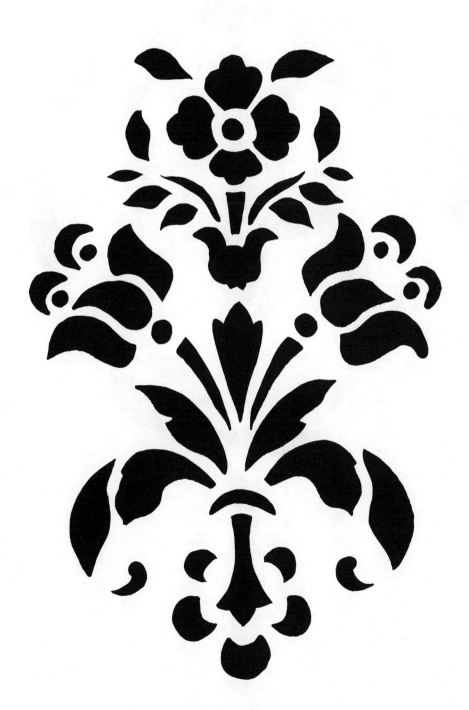

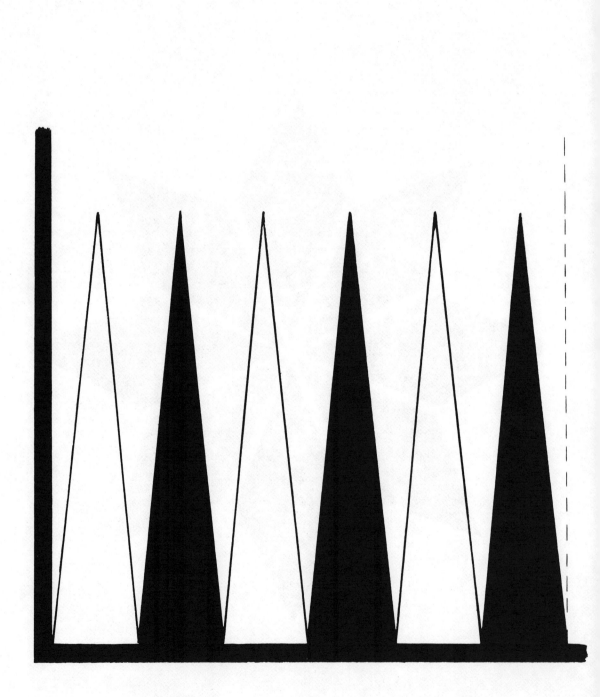

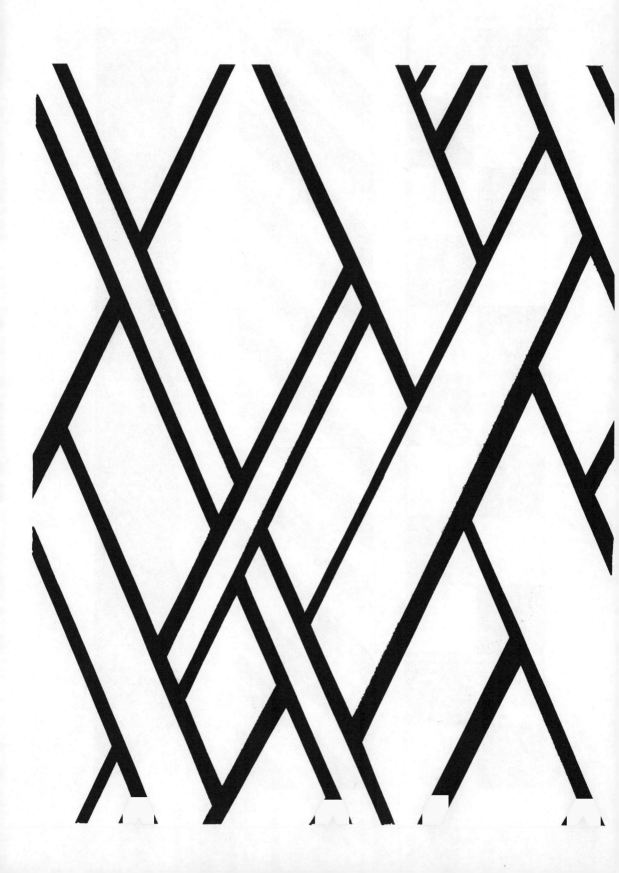

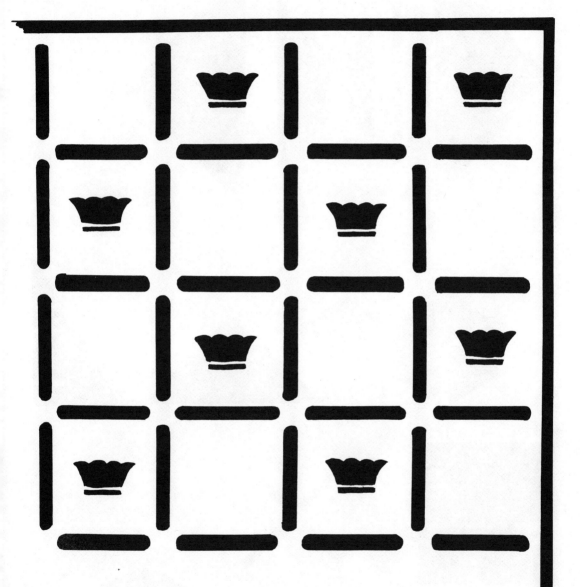

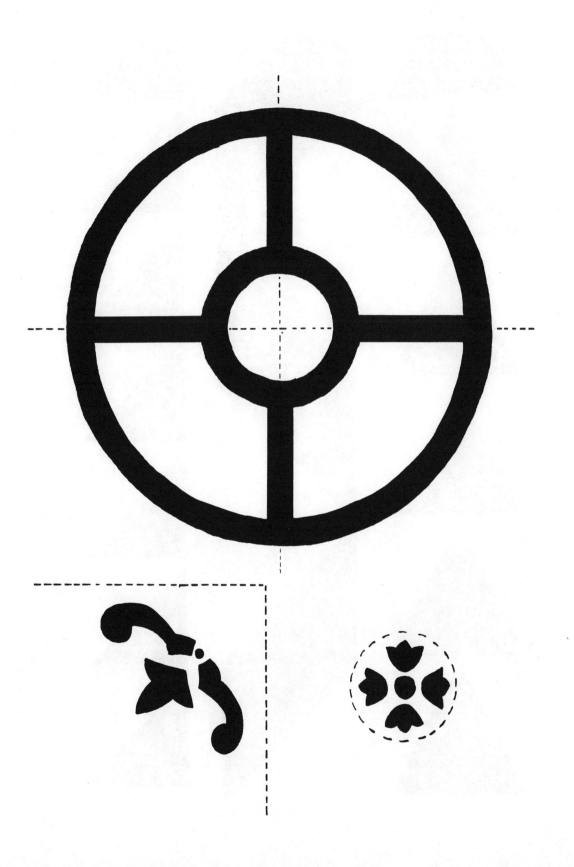

ABCDE
FGHIJ
KLMN
OPQRS
TUVW
XYZ

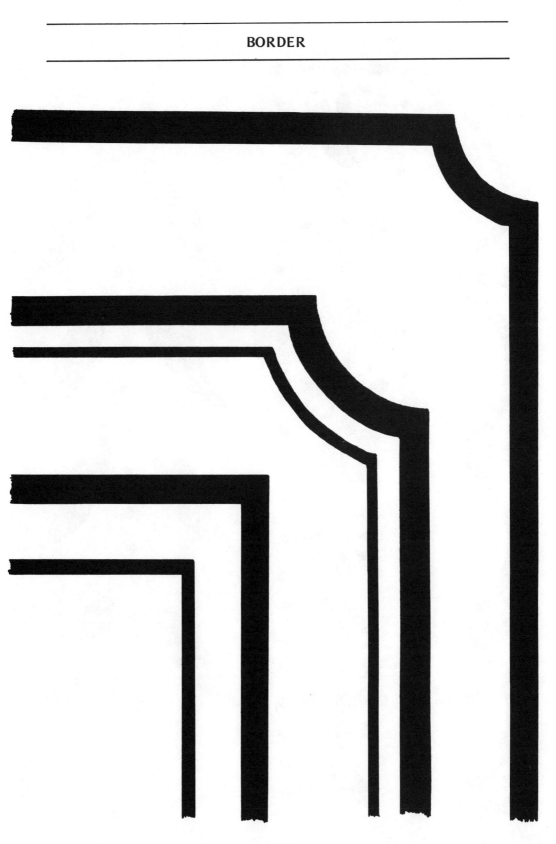

133

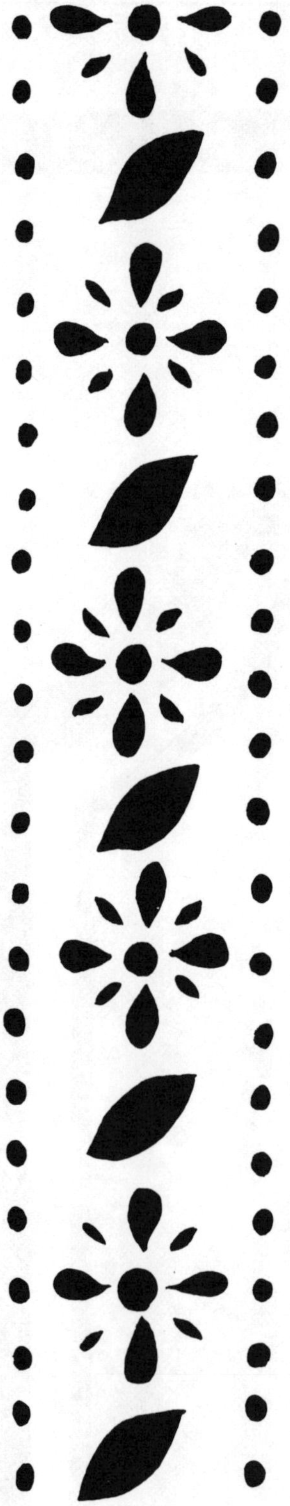

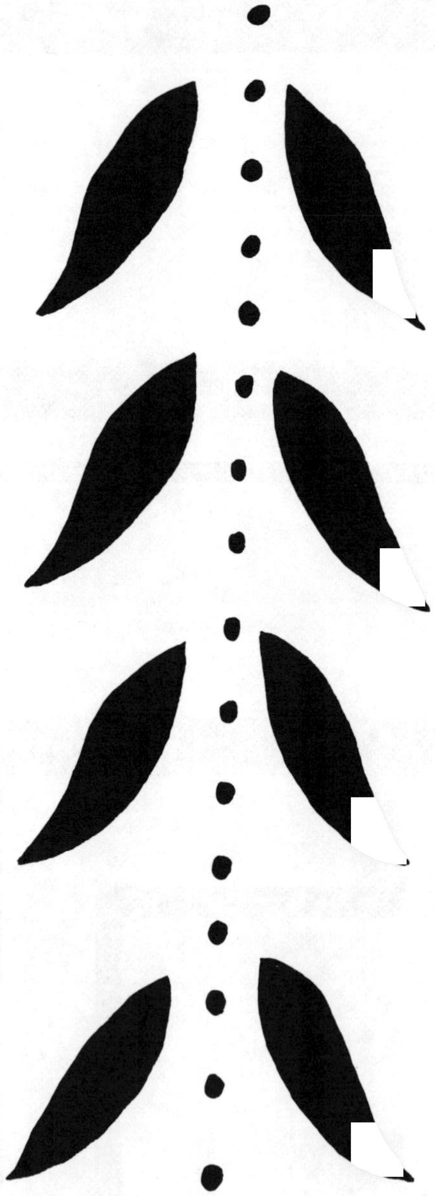

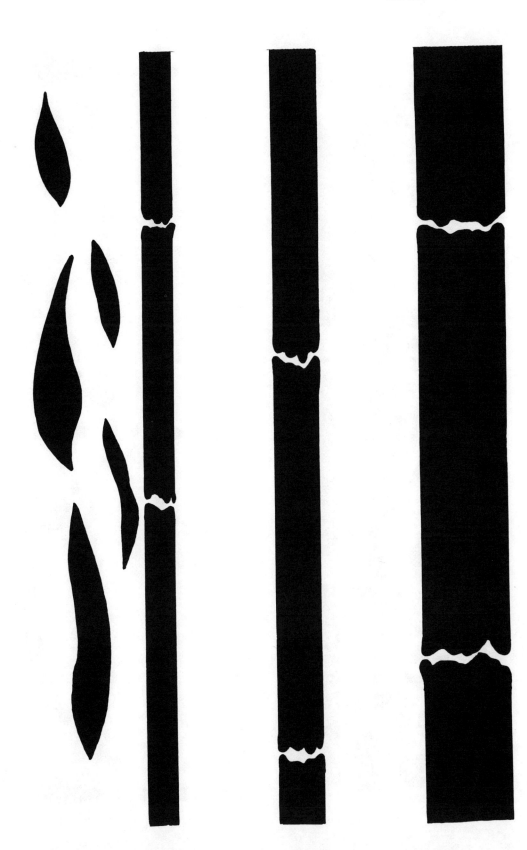

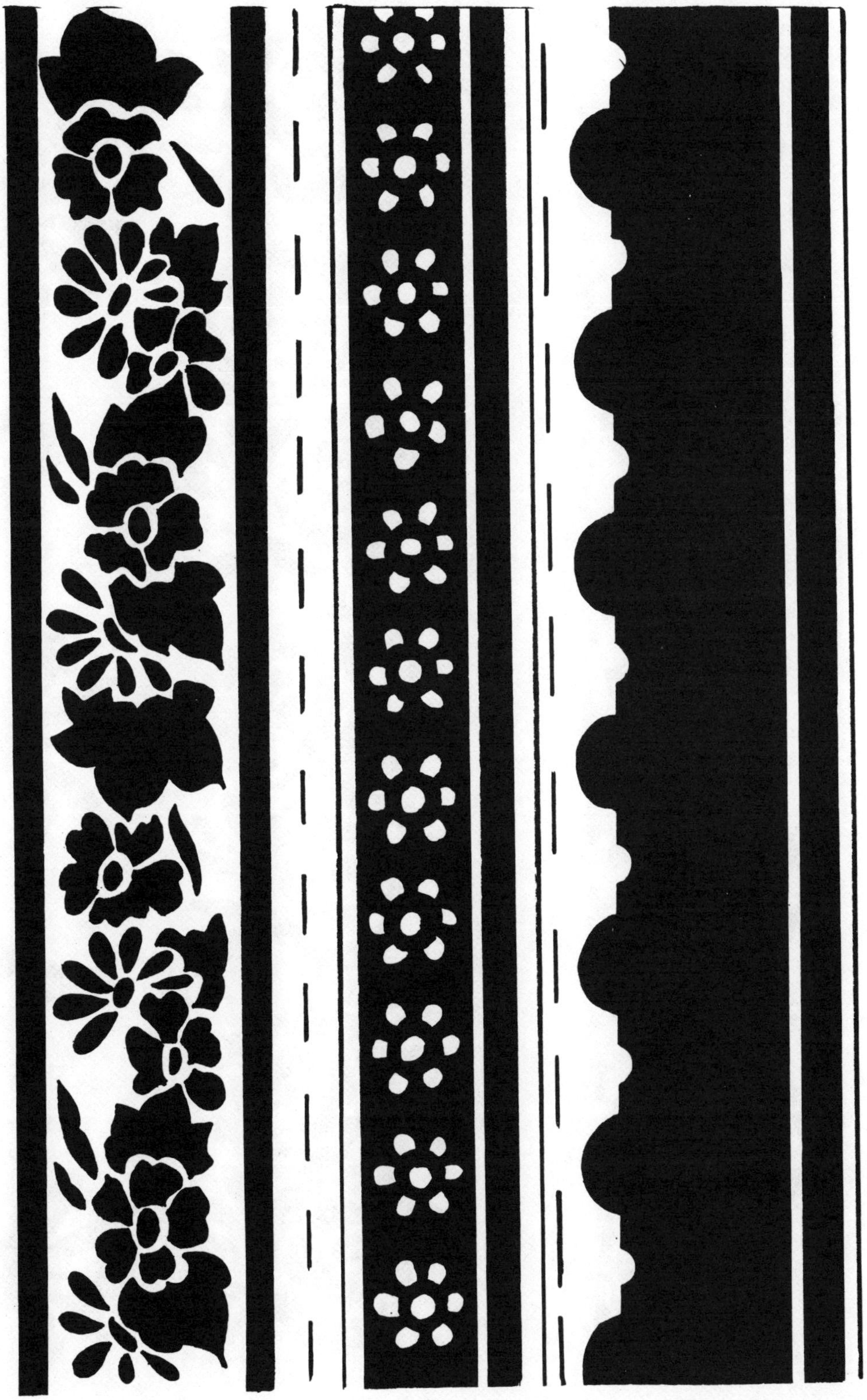

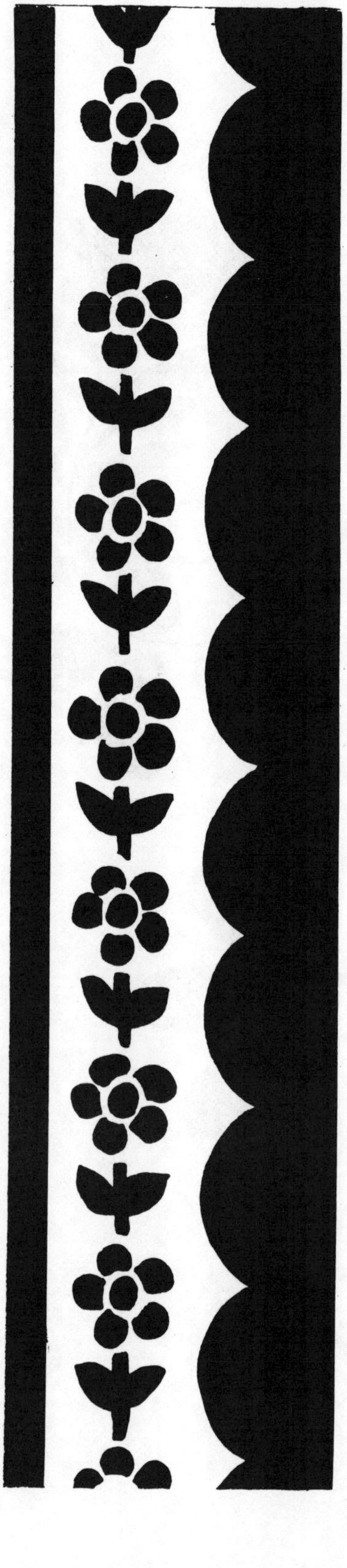

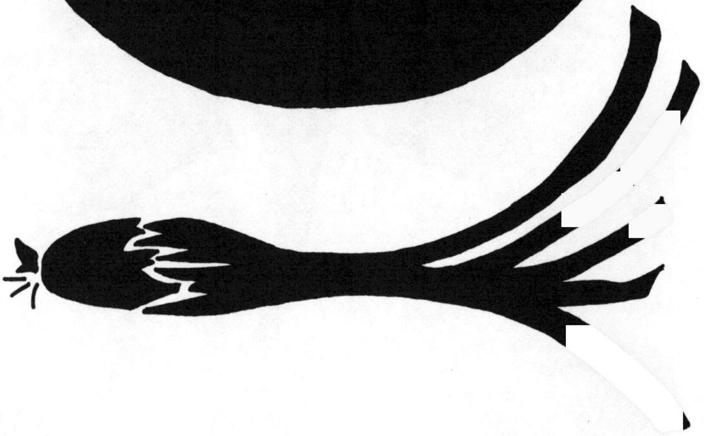

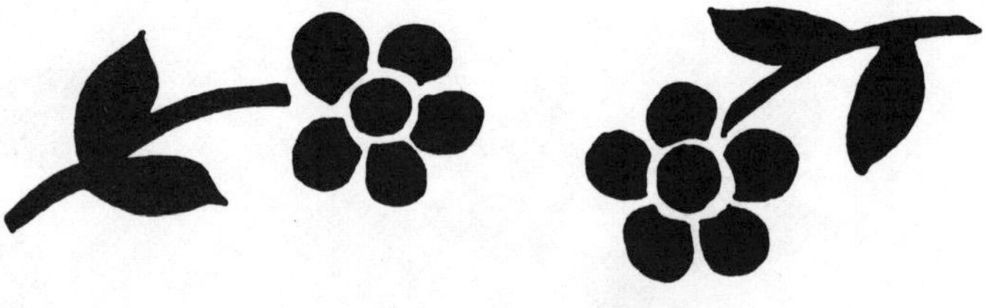

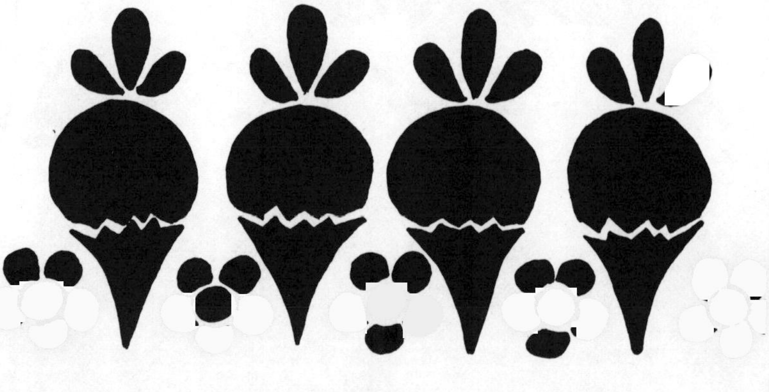

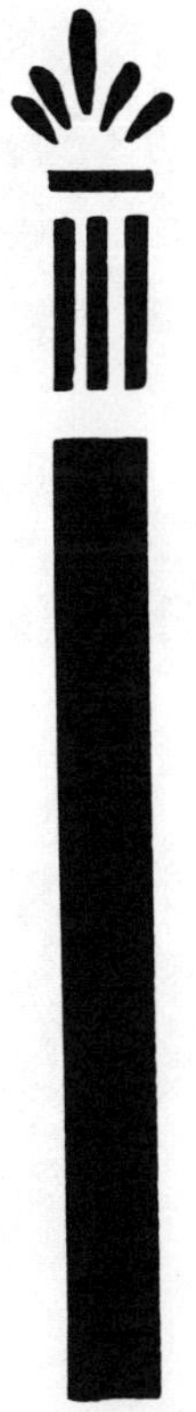

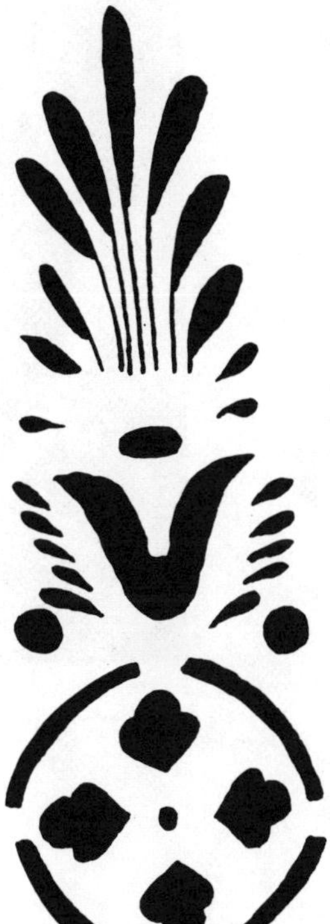

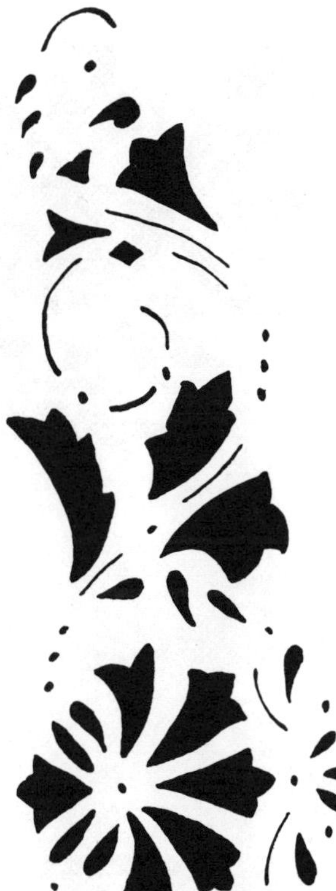

# INDEX